Captain Kirk ar ... trapped on the ...

A planet that ha ... culture after the ...style life of the Chicago mobs of the 1920 s.

Where arguments are settled by shoot-outs, leaders are called Bosses and enemies are outfitted with cement overshoes.

When Kirk and Spock are given an offer they can't refuse, the Feds are cut in for...

A PIECE OF THE ACTION

OTHER **STAR TREK FOTONOVELS**™
YOU WILL ENJOY—

STAR TREK™*

A PIECE OF THE ACTION

written by **DAVID P. HARMON**
and **GENE L. COON**

adapted from the television series
created by **GENE RODDENBERRY**

BANTAM BOOKS · TORONTO · NEW YORK · LONDON

RLI: $\dfrac{\text{VLM 6 (VLR 5–7)}}{\text{IL 5}+}$

A PIECE OF THE ACTION
A Bantam Book / June 1978

Designed and produced by
Michael Parrish, Los Angeles

Star Trek™ *designates a trademark of*
Paramount Pictures Corporation.

Fotonovel™ *designates a trademark of*
Mandala Productions.

ISBN 0-553-12022-0

Published simultaneously in the United States and Canada

Bantam Books are published by Bantam Books, Inc. Its trademark, consisting of the words "Bantam Books" and the portrayal of a bantam, is registered in the United States Patent Office and in other countries. Marca Registrada. Bantam Books, Inc., 666 Fifth Avenue, New York, New York 10019.

PRINTED IN THE UNITED STATES OF AMERICA

0 9 8 7 6 5 4 3 2 1

From The Office of the President
of Sigma Iotia II

Dear Mandala,

I just had a look at your Fotonovel about what happened up here on Sigma Iotia II with your Fed guys. The book was real nice. I especially liked all the shots of me and my boys. It was great remembering the old days, but the present ain't bad either. The Federation has sent us a whole bunch of your history books and so we've made a lot of changes. You know, we Iotians are pretty adaptable. Right now bobby-socks are the rage among our teenagers and I'm sporting a terrific crew cut.

When that Kirk guy first proposed the new arrangement, you'll remember that I was the first to agree. Hey, I'm no dummy. You don't cross a guy who has that kind of muscle backing him up.

I read a book about your government and I really enjoyed it, especially the part about having a president. So I held an election myself. Modesty prevents me from telling you what a landslide I won. I'm considering holding another one next year and I'm even thinking about having an opponent this time.

Oh, by the way, I made Jo Jo Krako Vice President. It's worked out great. I've never heard a word about him since. Yeah, things are going pretty good here. No wars, no inflation, no unemployment. There's some crime, but you can only teach old dogs so many new tricks.

As for me personally, I've given up the ways of my misspent youth—no more pool playing. Now I mostly spend my leisure time water skiing and with my family—yeah, I got married. Nice girl, too.

We've been working on the transtator thing the Feds left and my boys say they'll figure it out in a few more years and then we'll be able to travel all over the galaxy. I, myself, am looking forward to coming down to your Earth. I particularly am interested in visiting a place called Las Vegas. Sounds like my kind of town.

Well, that's about it—good luck to you and if you ever need a bunch of double-breasted suits, just give me a call.

Regards,
Bela Okmyx

The above letter was forwarded to us by Anthony Caruso, the well-known and versatile actor who has become a close personal friend of Mr. Okmyx over the years.

CAST LIST
The Feds:

James T. Kirk, Captain
William Shatner

A man whose independent nature and compassionate heart make him a natural leader. His overriding concern is always the well-being of his ship and its crew.

Spock, First Officer
Leonard Nimoy

Chief Science Officer. Of Vulcan and Terran heritage, which accounts for his analytical mind and extraordinary strength. Logic and reason rule his life.

Leonard McCoy, M.D., Lt. Commander
DeForest Kelley

Senior Ship's Surgeon, head of Life Sciences Department. Though surrounded by the most advanced equipment the Federation can offer, he still practices medicine more with his heart than his head.

Montgomery Scott, Lt. Commander
James Doohan

Chief Engineer. Unchallenged in his knowledge of the ship's engineering equipment. A veritable magician when it comes to seemingly impossible repairs.

Uhura, Lt. Communications Officer

Nichelle Nichols

Pavel Chekov, Ensign

Walter Koenig

Navigator

Hadley, Lieutenant

William Blackburn

Officer on the Bridge

The Iotians:

Bela Okmyx
Anthony Caruso
Boss of the Northside Territory

JoJo Krako
Victor Tayback
Boss of the Southside Territory

Kalo
Lee Delano
Okmyx's Goon

Zabo
Steve Marlo
Krako's Goon

Tepo
John Harmon
One of the minor bosses

Young Con Artist
Sheldon Collins

Krako's Gun Moll
Marlys Burdette

Krako's Hood
Buddy Garion

Mirt
Jay Jones

Girls on the Street
Dyanne Thorne
Sharyn Hiller

A PIECE OF THE ACTION

SPACE:

THE FINAL FRONTIER

THESE ARE THE VOYAGES
OF THE STARSHIP
"ENTERPRISE." ITS
FIVE YEAR MISSION: TO
EXPLORE STRANGE NEW
WORLDS...TO SEEK OUT
NEW LIFE AND NEW CIVI-
LIZATIONS ... TO
BOLDLY GO WHERE NO MAN
HAS GONE BEFORE.

CAPTAIN'S LOG:

STARDATE 4598.0

IN RESPONSE TO A CONVEN-
TIONAL RADIO SIGNAL TRANS-
MITTED ONE HUNDRED YEARS
BEFORE BY THE USS "HORI-
ZON," SHORTLY BEFORE BEING
LOST WITH ALL HANDS, WE ARE
EN ROUTE FOR SIGMA IOTIA
II, AN INHABITED PLANET ON
THE OUTER REACHES OF THE
GALAXY.

As always, with the *Enterprise* in planetary approach mode, the mood on the bridge is alert, expectant.

Approaching Sigma Iotia II, Captain.

Standard

Captain, I have achieved vocal contact with an official station. They've relayed us to a man named Okmyx. His title is Boss.
Boss? All right, Lieutenant, put him on.

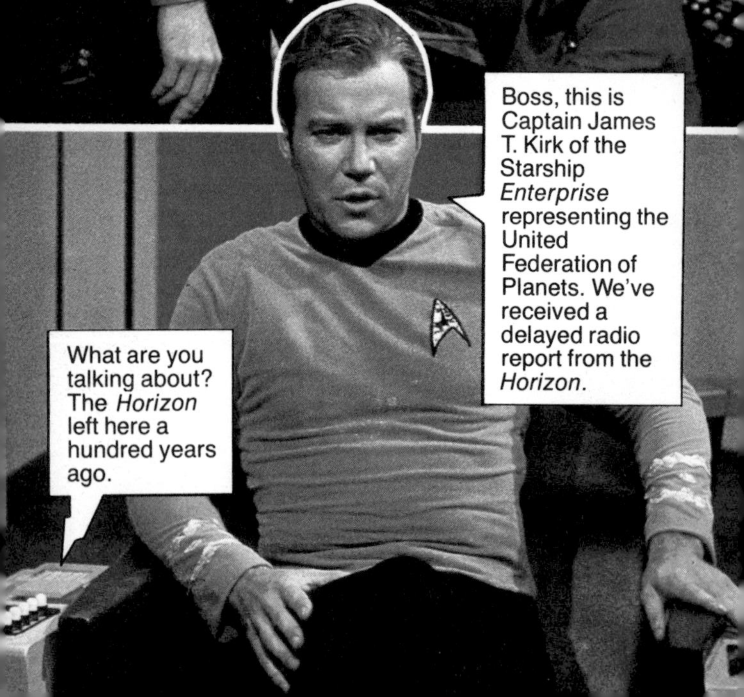
Boss, this is Captain James T. Kirk of the Starship *Enterprise* representing the United Federation of Planets. We've received a delayed radio report from the *Horizon*.
What are you talking about? The *Horizon* left here a hundred years ago.

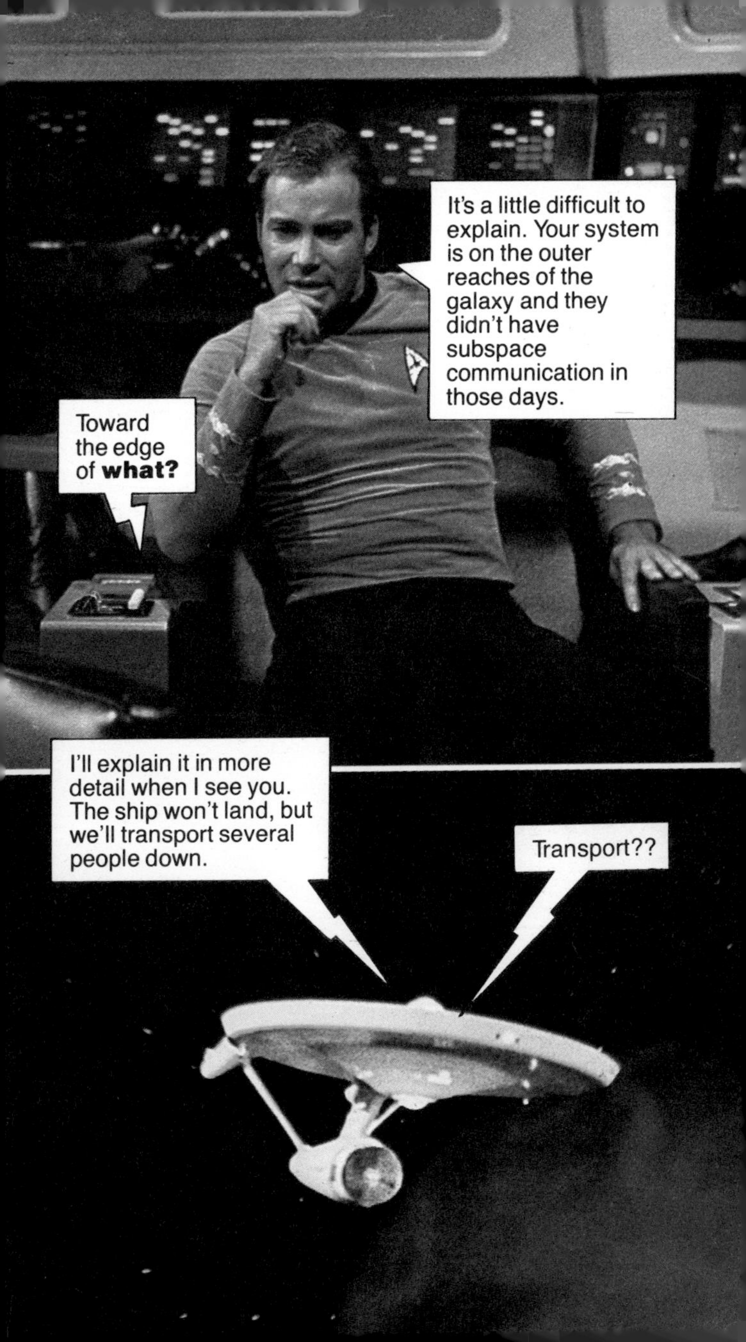
It's a little difficult to explain. Your system is on the outer reaches of the galaxy and they didn't have subspace communication in those days.
Toward the edge of **what?**
I'll explain it in more detail when I see you. The ship won't land, but we'll transport several people down.
Transport??

Don't worry. I promise to explain everything. Now then, where would it be convenient for us to meet?

Well, there's an intersection at the end of the block near a yellow fire plug.

Ah—Scotty, do you have coordinates for a yellow fire plug?

Located, sir.

Mr. Okmyx, we have your intersection located. Will five minutes be all right?

Fine. I'll have a reception committee there to meet you.

As First Officer Spock and Chief Surgeon McCoy enter the bridge, Captain Kirk hustles them back into the turbo-lift with orders to accompany him to Sigma Iotia II.

The *Horizon's* contact came before the interference directive went into effect.

Then they must have interfered with the normal evolution of the planet.

It will be interesting to see the results of the contamination.

But we do know that the Iotians are extremely intelligent and imitative.

We don't know that there is contamination. The evidence is only circumstantial.

In the Transporter Room, Kirk, Spock and McCoy receive standard equipment in preparation for immediate beam-down.

It sounds to me as if we're going down to recontaminate them!

If the damage has been done, Doctor, we are here to repair it.

Let's not argue about it. Let's go study it.

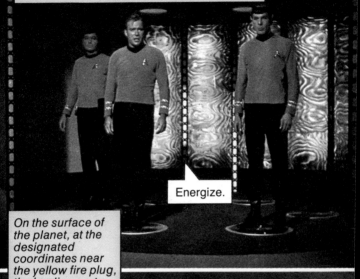

Taking their places in the Transporter, they await the matter-to-energy scrambling effect.

Energize.

On the surface of the planet, at the designated coordinates near the yellow fire plug, the landing party shimmers into existence...

...to materialize fully a moment later...

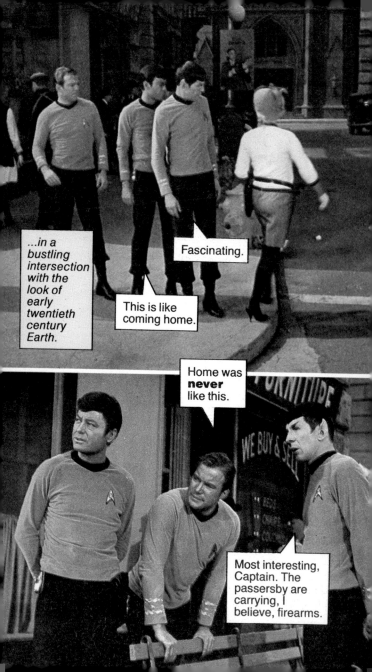

Suddenly the observers find themselves the focus of beligerent attention.
O.K., you three, let's see you **petrify.**
Sir, would you mind explaining that statement?
I want to see you turn to stone. Give me those gadgets you got on your belts, then put your hands over your head, or you ain't gonna have no heads to put your hands over.

Sir, we were asked to come down here by a Mr. Okmyx. He said—

I know what he said, bud. He said some of the boys would meet you. O.K., we're meeting you.

Well, those firearms are not necessary.

Well, since this Okmyx asked us down here, don't you think we should see him?

All right, get moving down this street.

As they turn to leave, an open touring car roars down the street, its passengers spraying the sidewalk with a hail of bullets.
Kirk, Spock and McCoy dive for cover as their captors exchange fire with the gunmen in the speeding car.

Is this how you greet all your guests?
It happens, pal.
NO PARKING
NO COMMERCIAL
ICE CREAM

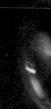

The black phaeton disappears around the corner and the fusillade is over as quickly as it began, leaving one man dead on the street.

Slightly shaken by their abrupt introduction to local customs, Kirk, Spock and McCoy exchange rueful glances as they peel themselves off the street.

Sir, there are several questions I would like to ask.

Then ask the Boss. I don't know nothin'. Now, get moving.

That's the contamination you're looking for, Jim.

Yes, but the *Horizon*'s crew weren't cold-blooded killers. And they didn't report finding this type of culture, either. Something has happened here.

A few steps later their progress is once again impeded, but this time by someone slightly more friendly.
Hey, Kalo, when's the Boss gonna do something about the crummy streetlights around here?
A girl ain't safe.
Yeah, and what about the laundry pick up? We ain't had a truck by in three weeks.
Write the Boss a letter.

At his headquarters, Bela Okmyx, "The Boss," is apprised of the capture of the landing party.

All right! Bring 'em in.

The captives are ushered in to find Okmyx positioned casually at his pool table.

Which one of you guys is the Captain?

That depends.

Make yourself a drink, Captain. It's good stuff. I distill it myself. Then grab yourself a cue.

Kalo, put that chopper down. These guys are our **guests.**

You gotta excuse my boys, but you can't be too careful around here these days.

Boss of the biggest territory in the world. But when you're the biggest, there's always some punk trying to cut you out. That's why we're so careful.

You mean you're the government around here?
What government? I got the biggest territory and I run it. It's just a matter of time until I burn all the other small-time operators.

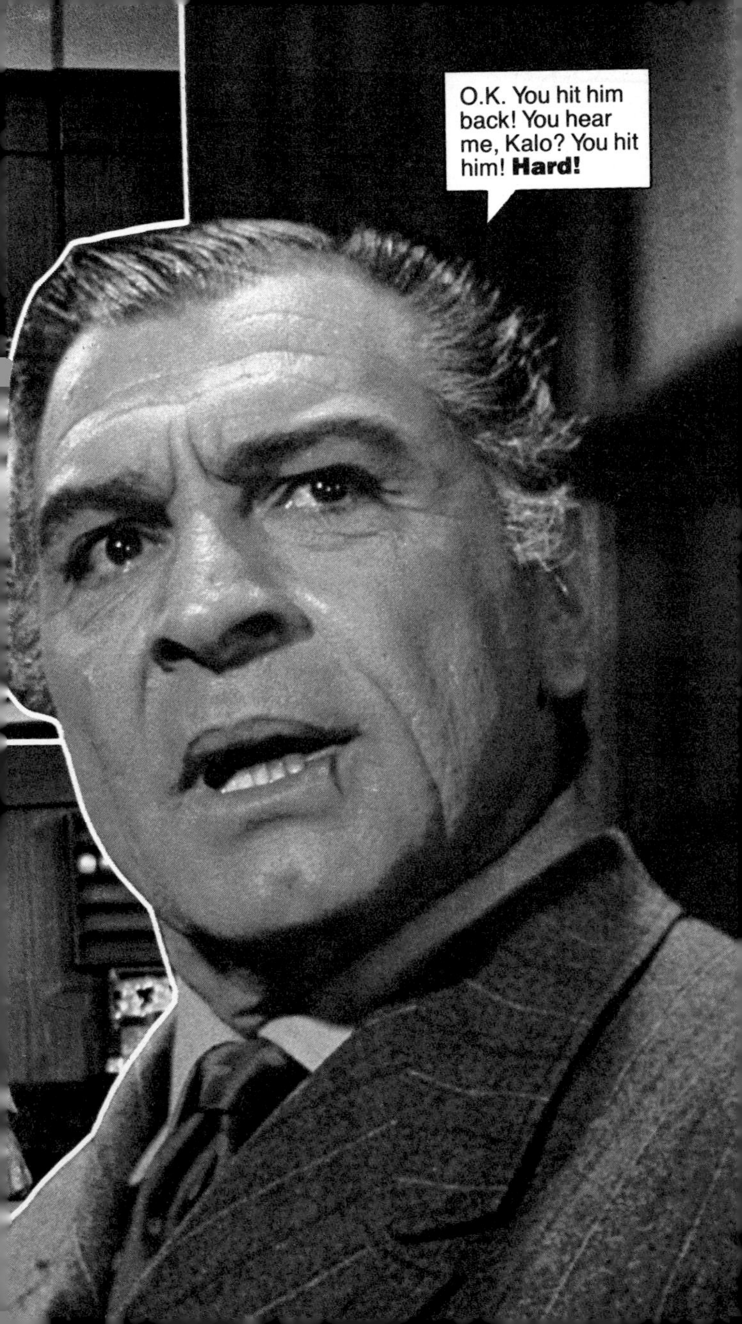
O.K. You hit him back! You hear me, Kalo? You hit him! **Hard!**

Surveying their surroundings, Spock's attention is drawn to a book, occupying a prominent position in the room.

Chicago Mobs of the Twenties

Captain. Doctor. I believe you should take a look at this.

This **could** be the key.

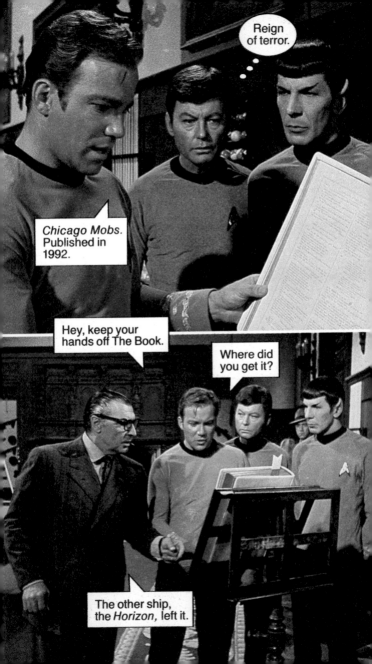

Didn't the *Horizon*'s crew leave any other books?
Sure, some textbooks on how to make radio sets and stuff like that. But I brought you down here so you could help me, not for you to ask questions.

What exactly do you want?

Well, I was thinking, pal, you Feds must have made a lot of improvements since that other ship came here. You probably got all kinds of fancy heaters up there.

So, here's the deal. You give me enough heaters to knock off all those other punks, then I'll take over and all you'll have to deal with is me.
Let me get this straight. You want the Federation to supply you with arms and assistance so you can carry out an aggression against your neighbors?

From now on you're gonna take orders from **me.** I'm gonna give you eight hours to give me what I want.

If I don't have the heaters by then, I'm gonna call your ship and have 'em pick you up... in a box. Understand?

A heater, huh? Let's see how good it works.

Hey, Boss, we picked up some stuff on these guys. This here's a heater. I don't know what the little boxes are.
Don't do that. You could knock out the side of this building.
That good, huh? Terrific. O.K., give me a hundred of these fancy heaters and we'll have no more trouble.
That's out of the question.

I'm warning you, Kirk, I usually get what I want and you're pushing your luck. Now, tell me, what's this other thing?

Reluctant to reveal the function of the communicators, their only link with the Enterprise, Kirk remains silent as Spock and McCoy, following his lead, feign indifference.

Kalo, take 'em to the warehouse and put 'em in the bag. Keep a sharp eye on 'em, you hear?
Yea, Boss, in the bag.
Come on. **Move it.**
As Kirk, Spock and McCoy are removed to the warehouse under guard, Bela Okmyx uses a captured communicator to attempt contact with the Enterprise.
Hey, you in the ship up there!

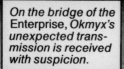

On the bridge of the Enterprise, Okmyx's unexpected transmission is received with suspicion.

I don't like the sound of this.

Scott here. Who is this?

This is Bela Okmyx. I got your Captain and his friends down here. If you want to see 'em alive again, send me down a hundred of those fancy heaters you got and some troops to show me how to use them.

Am I to understand that you're holding the Captain and his party?
You heard right, pal. And I'm gonna give you just eight hours to give me the goods I want or I put the hit on your friends. Understand?
I don't know. Scott out.

SHIP'S LOG:

STARDATE 4598.2

CHIEF ENGINEER SCOTT RE-
CORDING. ORBITING SIGMA
IOTIA II. THE CAPTAIN,
FIRST OFFICER AND CHIEF
SURGEON HAVE BEAMED TO THE
PLANET. WE HAVE RECEIVED A
TRANSMISSION FROM SOMEONE
CALLING HIMSELF BELA OKMYX
WHO DEMANDS A RANSOM OF ONE
HUNDRED TYPE I HAND PHASERS
IN RETURN FOR THE LIVES OF
OUR LANDING PARTY. WE HAVE
BEEN GIVEN EIGHT HOURS IN
WHICH TO COMPLY.

In the warehouse on Sigma Iotia II, as their guards become absorbed in a game of cards, the prisoners are allowed to speak privately.

It's amazing. One book on the gangs of old Chicago did all this.

Evidently, they used that one book as the blueprint for their entire society.

And, in old Chicago, conventional government almost broke down. The gangs nearly took over.

Well, this Okmyx is the worst gangster of all.

We may quarrel about Mr. Okmyx's methods, but his goal is essentially the correct one. This society must become united, or it will degenerate into total anarchy.

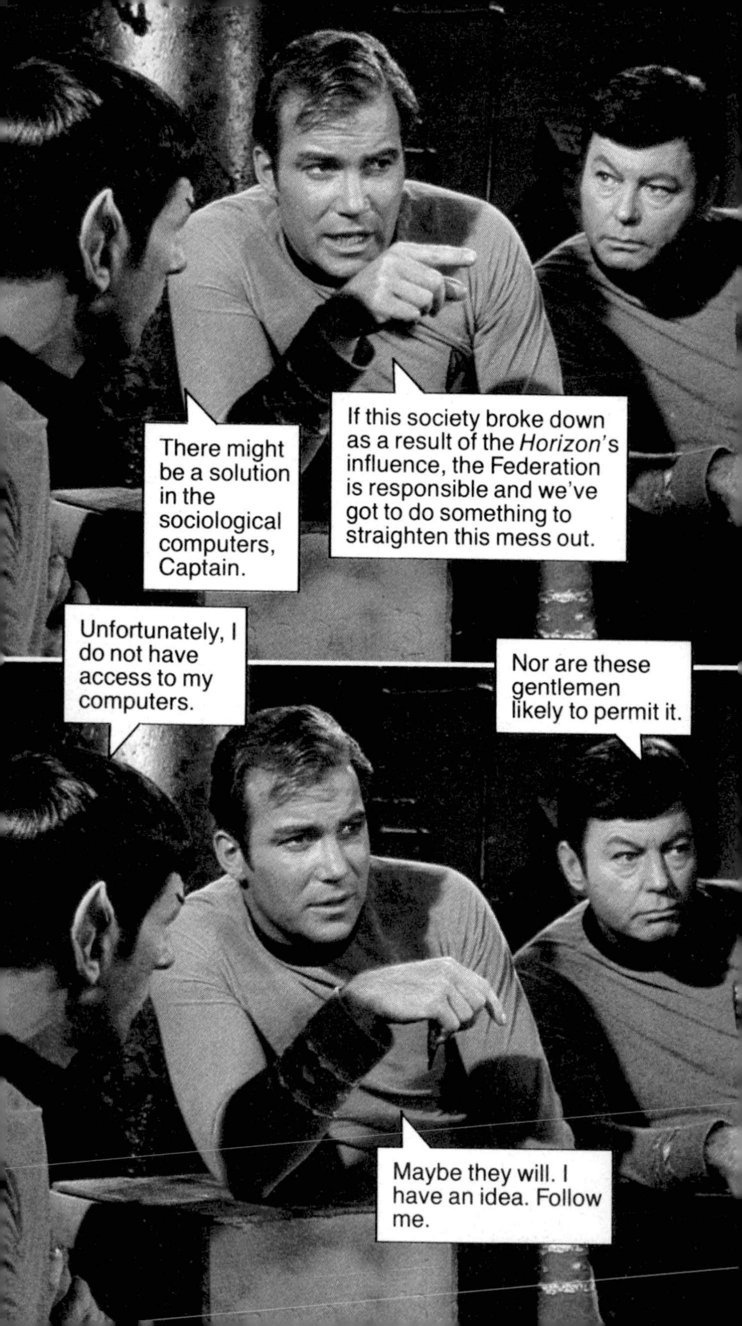
If this society broke down as a result of the *Horizon*'s influence, the Federation is responsible and we've got to do something to straighten this mess out.
There might be a solution in the sociological computers, Captain.
Unfortunately, I do not have access to my computers.
Nor are these gentlemen likely to permit it.
Maybe they will. I have an idea. Follow me.

Gentlemen, you know this game you're playing is for kids.

Yea? You think so?

I sure do. Now, on Beta Antares IV they play a man's game. But it's probably a little beyond you. It requires intelligence.

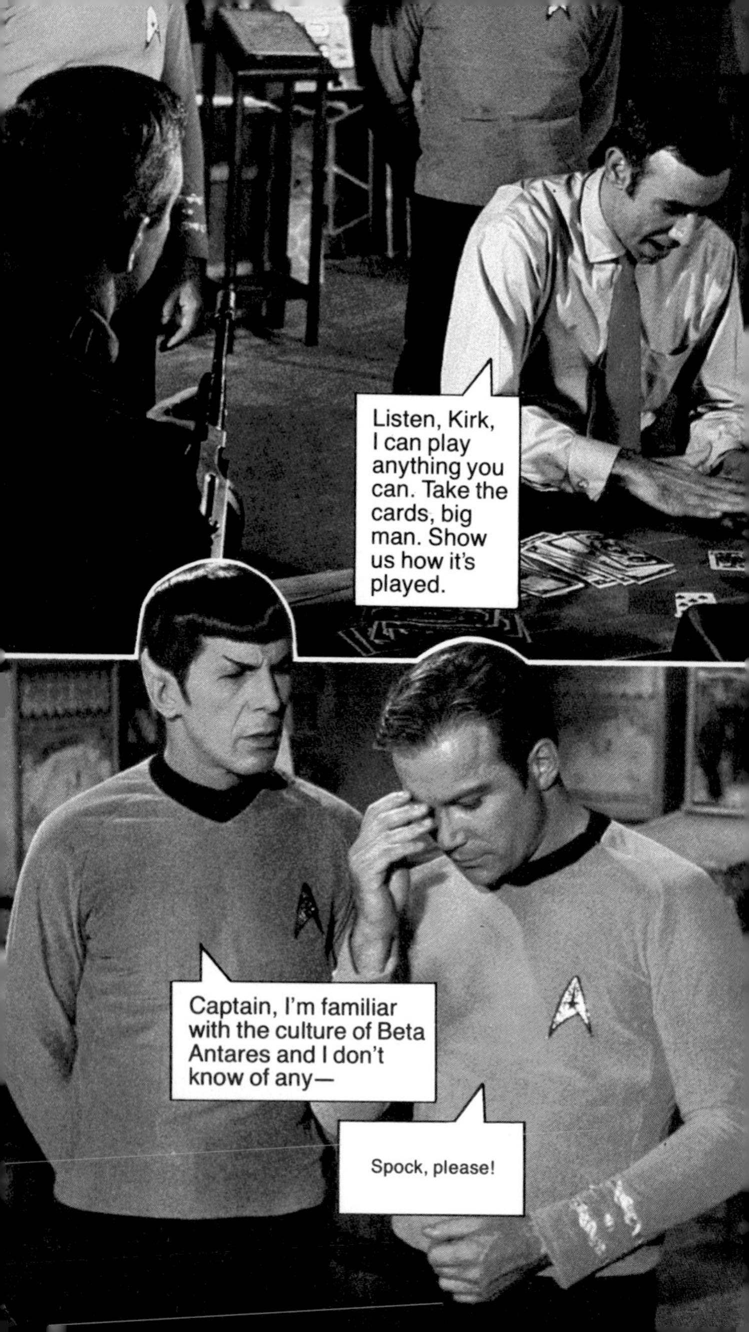
Listen, Kirk, I can play anything you can. Take the cards, big man. Show us how it's played.
Captain, I'm familiar with the culture of Beta Antares and I don't know of any—
Spock, please!

O.K. gentlemen, the name of this game is...uh... Fizzbin. That's right, Fizzbin.
Fizzbin? Never heard of it.
Really? Well, it's not too difficult. Each player gets six cards, except the dealer...uh... the player on the dealer's right. He gets . . . eh . . . seven.

The second card is turned up except on Tuesday. Look what you've got! Two jacks. You already have a Half-Fizzbin.
So, all I need is another jack?
No! If you got another jack you'd have a... a... Shralk. You'd be disqualified. What you need is a king and a deuce, except at night, when you'd need a queen and a four.
Except at night. I got it!

This should prove to be the most interesting game of Fizzbin I've ever seen.
Indeed!
Now, look what you got. Another jack. How lucky you are. If you had gotten a king, why then you'd get another card, except when it's dark, when you'd have to give it back.

You mean if it's dark on a Tuesday?
Yea, but what you're after is a Royal Fizzbin. But the odds against getting a Royal Fizzbin are astronomical.
Say, Spock, what are the odds in getting a Royal Fizzbin?
I've never computed them, Captain.

Well, they're astronomical, believe me. Now, for the last card. We'll call it the...eh... Kronk. You got it so far, Kalo?
Huh?!?!?

On cue, Spock applies the Vulcan nerve pinch, rendering the gangster unconscious.

The other gunmen are neatly dispatched by Kirk and Dr. McCoy who, if the occasion requires, knows how to hospitalize a man.

Intent upon reaching Okmyx before he can do any harm with the captured phasers, Kirk hurries through the dingy alleys.

But unfortunately, Kirk has not acted fast enough.
Hold it! O.K., pally, we're going for a little ride.
If it's all the same with you, I'd rather walk.

Looking more like a hearse than a taxi, a long black car glides to a stop in front of them.
Be smart, fella. Get in and no tricks.
Come to think of it, a ride might be quite nice.
And Kirk is prodded unceremoniously into the back seat.
This **does** complicate things!

Having located an unoccupied studio in a radio station, Spock and McCoy attempt to make contact with the Enterprise.

How are you with primitive radio equipment?

It's very simple. Amplitude modulation transmission. Simply adjust the frequency, throw this switch and...

That was the Jailbreakers with their latest record. And this is "Request-Time," brought to you by Bang-Bang, the sweetest little automatic in the world.

I don't believe that's the *Enterprise*, Spock.

Making another adjustment, Spock tries again.

Enterprise, this is Mr. Spock.

This time he is successful. On board the Enterprise, Communications Officer Uhura, monitoring the planet's radio broadcasts, picks up Spock's transmission.

Lt. Uhura here, Mr. Spock. What are you doing on this frequency?

A very long and complicated story, Lieutenant. Notify the Transporter Room—two to beam up on these coordinates.

At precisely that moment, Kirk and his grim escort reach their destination.

The sentry posted at the door eyes the Starship Captain narrowly.

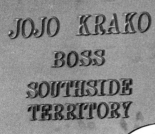

JOJO KRAKO
BOSS
SOUTHSIDE
TERRITORY

Only a punk or a creep would dress that way.

And inside, Jojo Krako, impatient to meet Kirk, kills time with a game of darts.

Eat dart, Okmyx!

Hi there, bud. I'm Jojo Krako. And you're the Fed. Well, well, well. Nice to meet ya.

Yeah, I want a deal. I want you to help me.

Hey, baby, go on over and help my guest relax. I'd like him to be real comfortable here.

Now, pal, what I want is—
Heaters, and troops to teach you how to use them. Then you'll attack the other bosses and take over the whole planet.
That's the general idea. You give me what I want and I'll cut you in for a third. Skimmed off the top. What do you think?

I've got a better idea. This planet has to be united. Let's contact the other bosses and sit down and talk about it like reasonable men.

Watch it, Kirk. The Book tells us how to handle things. O.K., honey, leave the man alone.

The Book tells us all about making hits. What do you think, we're **stupid** or something?
No, I don't think you're stupid, Mr. Krako. I just think your behavior is arrested.

I've never been arrested in my whole life. Listen, pally, I know how to get what I want. And if you want to live, you better come across.
I'm afraid I can't do that.

Hold him here, Zabo. Tell Cirl the Knife to sharpen up his blade. I just may have a job for him.

Too bad, fellow. Put him on ice, Zabo.

While on the
Enterprise,
Spock probes
the ship's
sociological
computers for a
solution to the
problem of
Sigma Iotia II.

Get anything on the computer?

No specifics. There is no record of any culture based on moral inversion.

You mean you're giving up?

No, Doctor. I'm merely saying the computers can offer us no logical way out of our current dilemma.

Huh? How'd you get back up there? Never mind. You'd better come back down. Krako's put a bag on your Captain.

I do not understand. Why would Mr. Krako put a bag on our Captain?

He kidnapped him, you dope. He'll scrag him too.

Look, you guys got something I want. I'll help you get your Captain back, then we can talk a deal.
I'm afraid I find it difficult to trust you, Mr. Okmyx.
What's to trust? Business is business. We'll call a truce. You come back down, my boys will spring Kirk and then we'll talk. O.K.?
You'll show no further hostility?

Hey, like I said, I'm a businessman. What do you say?
Since we must have our Captain back, I accept. We shall arrive in your office within ten minutes. Spock out.

Locked in a back room of Krako's headquarters, Kirk finds a radio... and formulates a plan.

This armature coil will make a nice trip-wire.

Having rigged the wire by the bottom of the door, Kirk grabs a blanket from the cot and attracts the attention of his guards.

Help! Help me! **Help!**

As the guards rush in and trip over the wire, Kirk bags, boggles and batters them to sleep.

I just might need this.

On the Enterprise, Spock and McCoy prepare for a rescue mission.
Mr. Scott, though we hope to avoid interference, I suggest you set one of our phaser banks on a strong stun position.

Aye, sir.
I trust we shall not have to use them, but it is best to be prepared.
Now you're beginning to make sense.

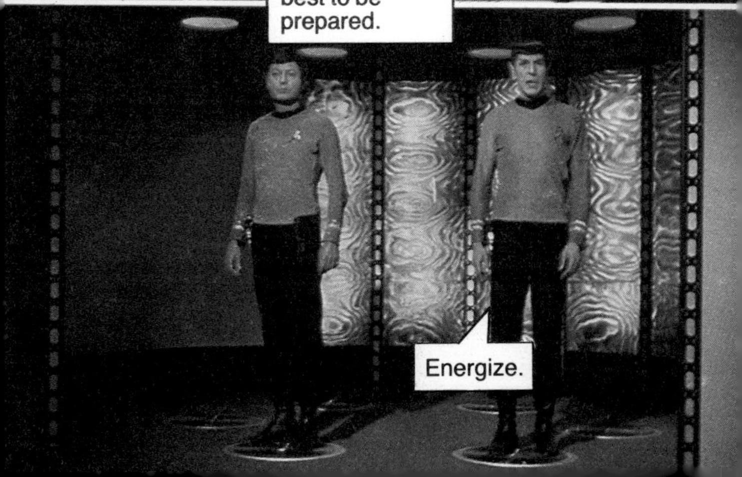
Energize.

On Sigma Iotia II, Bela Okmyx briefs his welcoming commitee.

You know what to do?

Don't worry, Boss. They can't do nothing 'til they're through sparkling.

Punctually, Spock and McCoy materialize in Mr. Okmyx's office.

It may be just as well. Did you find out anything from the computer?
Nothing useful. Logic and practical information do not seem to apply here.

You admit **that?**
To deny the facts would be illogical, Doctor.
Then you don't mind if I play a hunch?
I'm sanguine about hunches, Captain, but I have no practical alternative.
What do you have in mind, Jim?

A few moments later, a Starship Captain and his First Officer, the cream of Star Fleet's officer cadre, exit Okmyx's headquarters.

Key in the ignition. Ignition turned on. Starter pushed. But nothing's happening.
I believe they had a device known as a clutch. Perhaps it's one of those pedals on the floor.
With a bit of trial and error, they are under way.

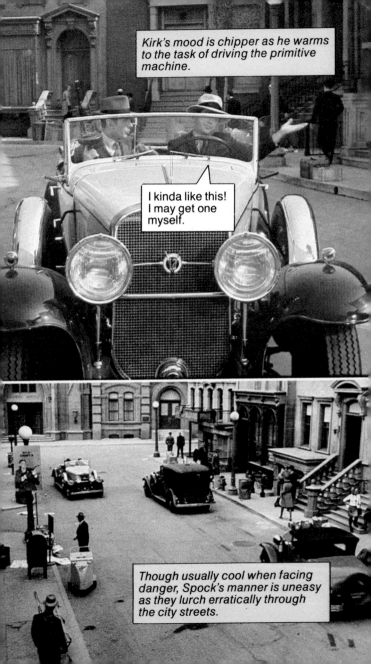

As Kirk and Spock ponder their strategy, they are accosted by a local small businessman.

It's a hit, ain't it? Can I watch?

Young man, run along and play.

You gonna try and hit Krako out here? You guys must be **nuts.** You open up and you'll be scragged from every window on the street.

Catching the sentries off guard, Kirk and Spock make short work of it.

Nice job. Now, what about me?

You said you wanted a piece of action and that's **exactly** what you got!

All right, no one on the street can see. We can use our phasers. Set yours for stun.

In the twinkling of an eye, two more of Krako's thugs are immobilized.

Well, ain't that nice. I was wondering how I was going to get you back and here you deliver yourselves.

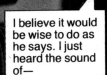

A few moments later, with the ad-vantage once again on Krako's side...
So this is the fancy heater, huh? Show me how it works.
Perhaps you'd like to discuss this in private. One of these could make any one of your boys a pretty big boss.
Hey, are you saying my boys can't be trusted?
Come to think of it, let's get some privacy.

Understanding the need for fast and certain communication, Kirk lapses smoothly into the local jargon.
All right, Krako, let's get down to business. You can forget about cutting us into your deal. That's peanuts to an outfit like the Federation.
Right?
Unquestionably.
I said "right."
Right!

Here's the picture, Krako. We're taking over. You cooperate with us and maybe we'll cut you in for a piece of the action.
How much?
A miniscule...uh... a very small piece.
How much is that?

Never mind. We'll figure it out later.
Hey, I thought you guys had laws. No interference.
Who's interfering? We're taking over! It's just that the Federation doesn't want to come in here and use our muscle. That ain't subtle.

What we do is, we help one guy take over the planet. He pulls the strings. Then we pull his. Get it?
What's your cut?

What do you care so long as you're being cut in? Of course, if you're not interested, we could always talk with Bela Okmyx.
Hey, who said I ain't interested? It's a deal. Go ahead. Call your ship. Bring down whatever you need.

Kirk to *Enterprise.*

Enterprise. Scott here.

Scotty, we made a deal with Krako. We're taking over the whole planet as soon as you're ready.

Do you think that's wise, sir?

Sure, we can trust Krako. We don't have any choice. You know what I mean? He's standing about twelve feet in front of me all ready to be our pal.
Scotty, I'd like to show him the ship, to show him we're on the level, but he would never allow it. You know how it is?
Aye, I know indeed. Ready when you give the word.

You may begin, Mr. Scott.

Jojo Krako's look of astonishment fades with him as the transporter beam takes hold.

Krako's henchmen remain bewildered just long enough...

...for Kirk and Spock to persuade them to "nap." Then they head back to Okmyx's territory.

Scotty stands ready to welcome Krako as he arrives in the Transporter Room of the Enterprise.

Hey, how did I get here? What happened?

Looks like we put the bag on you, doesn't it?

Wait a minute, I got rights.

You've got nothing. Now, mind your place or you'll be wearing concrete galoshes.

Huh? You mean cement overshoes?

Aye!

The Feds snatched Krako. I've never seen anything like it. They're planning on taking over. Bela's mixed up in it. I got a hunch they're headed over to his place now.

At Okmyx's place, McCoy's concern mounts.

All right, Okmyx, where's Captain Kirk and Mr. Spock?

Knowing Krako, he'll

Wrong again, Okmyx.

Now, listen up good. I'm getting sick and tired of playing pattycake with you penny ante operators. So, sit down and shut up.

Cover him, Spocko.

Right, Boss.

O.K., sweetheart, the Federation's moving in. If you don't play ball, you're out. All the way out. Know what I mean?
Yeah! Sure! Why didn't you say so in the first place? All you had to do was explain it.

Kirk to *Enterprise.* Scotty, you got Krako on ice?
Aye, he's here. Mad enough to chew neutronium, but behaving himself.
O.K., baby, cool it, till I flag you.

A short time later, after having assembled all the different gang bosses, Kirk announces his intentions.

From now on, the Federation's taking over. This planet's gonna be run like a business. That means you're gonna make a profit.

And what's **your** percentage?

I'm cutting the Federation in for forty percent. You got any objections?
Yeah. I hear a lot of talk, but all I see is you and a couple of your boys. I don't see no Federation.
Listen. They got a ship. Believe me. I was there.

At that moment, Krako's boys arrive in force. The street below erupts with the deadly stutter of machine-gun fire.
Hey, it's my boys. They're making a hit on this place
Don't get so excited. My boys'll put 'em down.

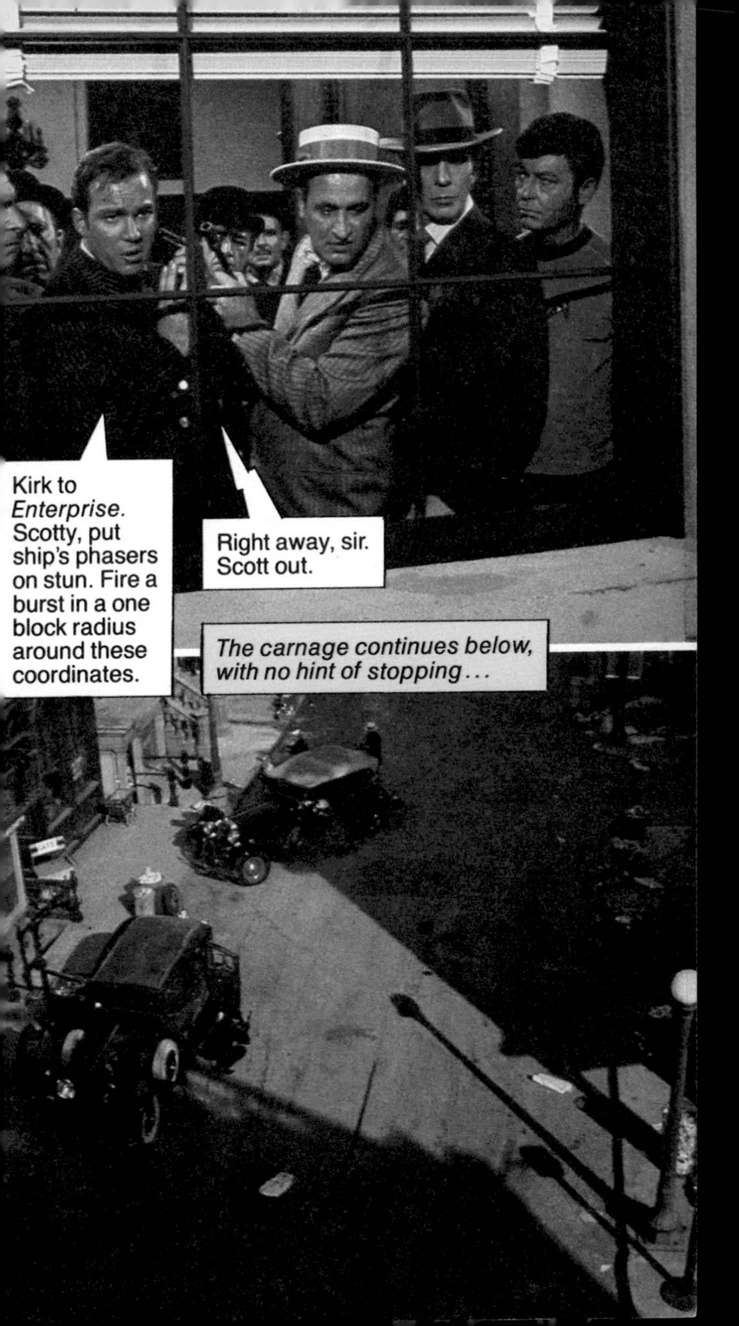
Kirk to *Enterprise.* Scotty, put ship's phasers on stun. Fire a burst in a one block radius around these coordinates.
Right away, sir. Scott out.
The carnage continues below, with no hint of stopping . . .

...when suddenly the streets are illuminated by a momentary, brilliant glare, punctuated by the indescribable throbbing of a starship's phasers.

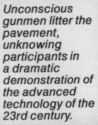

Unconscious gunmen litter the pavement, unknowing participants in a dramatic demonstration of the advanced technology of the 23rd century.

Now, are you ready to talk business or do I—
Hey, a syndicate makes sense to me. I'm a peaceful man at heart. I'm sick and tired of all these hits.
Like you said, there's too many bosses. We can't get anything done. I was thinking, if there was a Top Boss, maybe somebody like you...
Thanks anyway, but no. The Federation can't get connected with a small-time operation like this.

The way I see it is that you, Bela, would be the Top Boss and Krako would be your Lieutenant. And I don't want any trouble from the rest of you or you'll have to answer to the Feds. We'll be back every year to collect our cut.
Hey, look, you figure maybe forty percent is enough?

Hey, we ain't greedy. Forty percent should be sufficient.

Now, let's break out some of your drinking stuff, Mr. Okmyx, and celebrate the syndicate!

PERSONAL JOURNAL, CAPT. JAMES T. KIRK

STARDATE 4598.7

WE HAVE LEFT ORBIT AROUND SIGMA
IOTIA II AND THANKS TO A REMEDY
KNOWN TO BONES AND SCOTTY, HAVE
RECOVERED FROM THE EFFECTS OF MR.
OKMYX'S DRINKING STUFF. THE IO-
TIANS, HOWEVER, WILL NEED MORE
TIME TO RECOVER FROM THE EFFECTS
OF THE BOOK. A CULTURE CAN BEND
ONLY SO FAST WITHOUT BREAKING.
INEVITABLY, I AM MOVED TO SPECU-
LATE UPON THE DANGERS OF LIMITED
CULTURAL INFLUENCE AND THE
EFFECTS CERTAIN OTHER BOOKS MIGHT
HAVE HAD. THERE WAS SOMETHING PA-
THETIC YET APPEALING ABOUT THEIR
TECHNOLOGY.

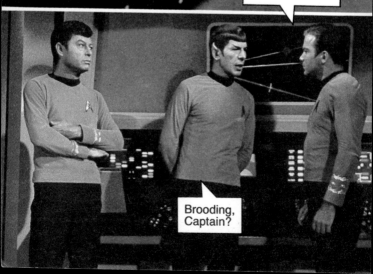

Brooding, Mr. Spock. A somber, emotional state. Now, do you wish to continue it, or are you going to discuss it?
Captain, I am neither brooding nor somber. But I do have some reservations about your solution to the problem of the Iotians.

To leave a criminal organization in charge is highly irregular, to say the least. I'm also curious as to how you propose to explain to Star Fleet Command that a starship must be sent each year to collect our cut.
Good question. I will propose that our cut be put into the planetary treasury and be used to guide the Iotians into a more ethical system.

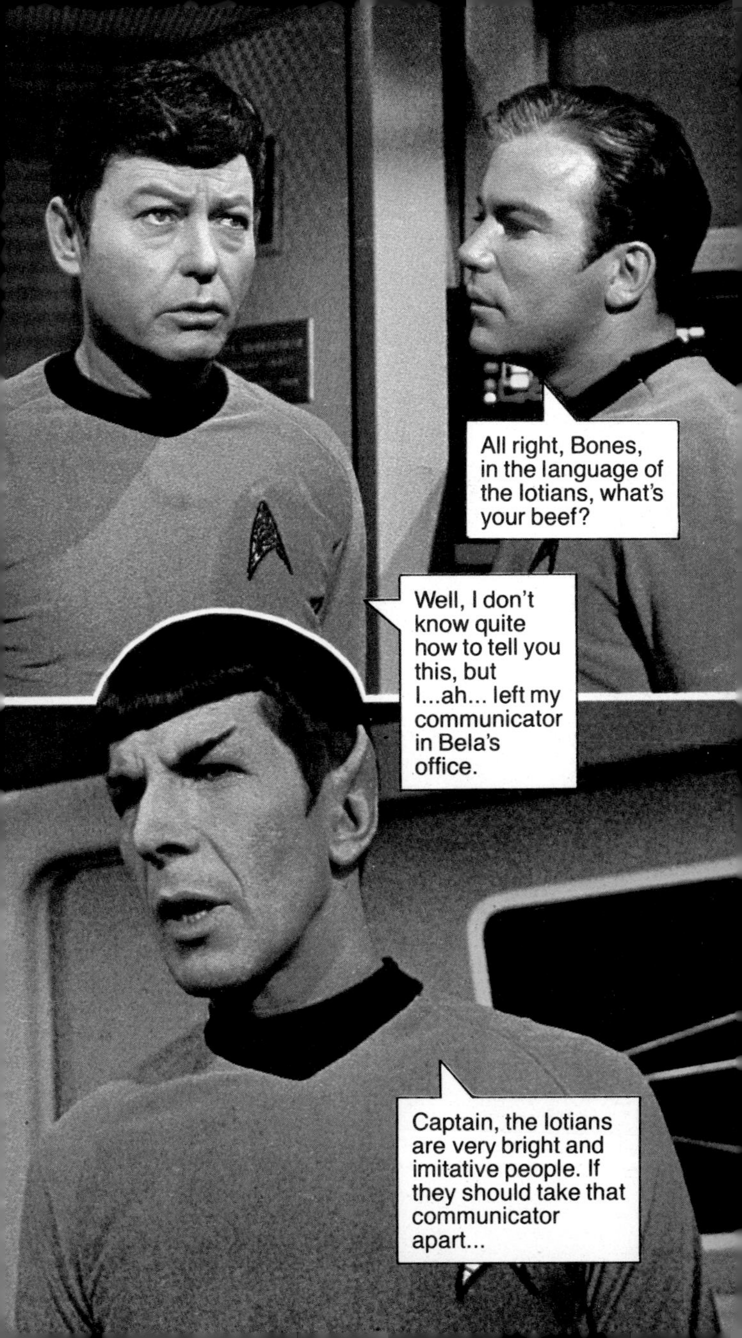
All right, Bones, in the language of the Iotians, what's your beef?
Well, I don't know quite how to tell you this, but I...ah... left my communicator in Bela's office.
Captain, the Iotians are very bright and imitative people. If they should take that communicator apart...

Certainly. In a few years, the Iotians may demand a piece of **our** action!

GLOSSARY

Armature—A piece of soft iron or steel that connects the poles of a magnet.

Communicator—Portable hand-held equipment used primarily for maintaining communication between landing parties on the surface of a planet and an orbiting Starship. Its outside grid functions as its antenna. When activated, it allows a transporter on the starship to pinpoint a person's exact location in order to be beamed aboard.

Fizzbin—An extremely difficult game indigenous to Beta Antares IV with rules fluctuating with the time of day, days of the week and, assumably, the credulousness of the other players.

Neutronium—An alloy so dense that it is impenetrable even by the Starship's phaser.

Phasers—Type I and II, personal hand-held weapons having adjustable settings including "stun," "dematerialize," "heat activation" and "kill." Though only worn by security men on board the Starship, they are often issued to all members of a landing party.

Ship's Log—Record-keeping method of all important activities aboard a Starship. Entries are made by the Captain and, in his absence, the Chief Officer in charge.

Sigma Iotia II—A planet located on the outer edge of the galaxy inhabited by extremely intelligent and highly imitative humanoids. Nothing is known of its previous culture, which was abandoned when it embraced the manners, vocabulary, dress and behavior of the gangs in Chicago circa 1920.

Transporter—A device used to move crew and/or cargo from the Starship to planets and back by changing the object's original molecular structure into energy which is beamed to a predetermined point where the original molecular formation is reconstructed.

Transtater—The technological basis for the Starship's transporters, phasers, communicators and every piece of important equipment used by the Federation.

Turbo-lift—Elevator-type compartments connecting all the decks of the Starship, capable of moving horizontally and vertically and operated either manually or by voice.

United Federation of Planets—Democratic alliance of planets comprised of several solar systems including Sol. All decisions affecting member planets are made through delegates to the Federation Council.

U.S.S. *Horizon*—A Federation vessel lost shortly after an exploratory mission to Sigma Iotia II. Its technical equipment was so limited that it didn't even have sub-space communication and had to rely on a conventional radio system for sending and receiving messages.

Vulcan Nerve Pinch—A method of temporarily immobilizing humanoids and rendering them unconscious, requiring both strength and knowledge of anatomy.

STAR TREK QUIZ #8

In each question below, circle the one answer that best completes the sentence.

1. A landing party is sent to Sigma Iotia to:

a. guide them into an ethical system of government.
b. find out what happened to the U.S.S. *Horizon*.
c. study their culture.
d. answer a call for assistance.

2. Kirk is reluctant to explain to Okmyx what a communicator is because:

a. the Iotians will then be able to develop their own transtators.
b. it's against Starfleet orders.
c. it's his only way to contact the *Enterprise*.
d. the Iotians will confiscate it.

3. When Kirk refuses to supply Okmyx with weapons, Okmyx threatens to:

a. use the captured phasers on Spock and McCoy.
b. bag him.
c. turn Kirk over to Krako's gang.
d. kill him.

4. Spock agrees with Mr. Okmyx that:

a. the Federation is responsible for contaminating the Iotian culture.
b. Mr. Okmyx is the only boss strong enough to run the country.
c. killing is never a logical solution to any problem.
d. all the territories must be united.

5. When playing Fizzbin, the player on the dealer's right gets:

a. seven cards.
b. seven cards except when it's dark.
c. seven cards except when it's Tuesday.

d. seven cards except when it's dark on Tuesday.

6. When playing Fizzbin, one always wants to avoid getting a:

   a. Kronk
   b. Shralk
   c. Half-Fizzbin
   d. Royal Fizzbin

7. Spock and McCoy are able to contact the *Enterprise*:

   a. when they recover their communicators.
   b. by using the Iotians' space tracking equipment.
   c. when Spock adjusts the Iotian primitive amplitude modulation to sub-space frequencies.
   d. because Uhura is monitoring all broadcasts.

8. The only thing Kirk does *not* experience is being:

   a. "bagged."
   b. "kidnapped."
   c. outfitted with "cement shoes."
   d. "put on ice."

9. Spock returns to Iotia:

   a. because Okmyx threatens Kirk's life.
   b. to persuade Okmyx to work for peaceful coexistence.
   c. when Krako tells him Kirk has been bagged.
   d. to talk to Krako.

10. Spock hesitates using the *Enterprise*'s phasers because:

   a. he is fearful he'll hurt Kirk.
   b. he hopes to avoid forceful interference.
   c. it is not a logical way to react.
   d. he has agreed to a truce.

Turn the page for the answers.

Deep within the planet Janus VI, hiding in the dark and shadowy labyrinth of tunnels, a savage, vengeful monster lurks. Having claimed the lives of fifty men, it waits for its next prey. Knowing not what it is, but ever conscious of what it can do, Kirk and Spock search the underground maze, and terror becomes their companion when they come face to face with...

THE DEVIL IN THE DARK

The next Star Trek Fotonovel—Available wherever paperback books are sold.